Call To Worship Note Takers Book

All Scripture is God- breathed and is useful for teaching, rebuking correcting and training in righteousness, so that the man of God may be thoroughly equipped for every good work."
~2 Timothy 3:16 - 17 NIV~

2nd Edition August 2016

Library of Catalog Cataloging-in-Publication Data, Nancy M.
Roundtree, Call to Worship Note Taker's Book, Notebook, Religion,
approximate pages 200

Printed in the USA

ISBN: 978-0-9978828-2-7

Giving honor to the God who is the head of my life, I dedicate this book to the Lord Jesus Christ.
There are no amounts of words or gratitude I can give you to express how thankful I am to you for loving me enough to die for me.
Thank you for using me as a vessel to share your word to your people.

~~~~~~~~~~~~~

Call To Worship Note Taker's Book

Content:

~~~~~~~~~~~~~

And the LORD answered me, and said, Write the vision, and make it plain upon tables, that he may run that readeth it.
Habakkuk 2:2

SERMON
NOTES
SECTION

_____

SERMON TITLE

_____

DELIVERER OF THE MESSAGE

_____

DATE

Scriptures Used: _____

_____

Notes

_____

_____

_____

_____

_____

_____

_____

_____

_____

_____

_____

_____

_____

_____

_____

_____

_____

_____

_____

_____

_____

_____

_____

_____

_____

_____

_____

_____

_____

_____

_____

_____

_____

_____

_____

_____

SUMMARY (WHAT DID I LEARN):

_____

_____

_____

"This is the day that the Lord has made. Let us rejoice and be glad in it" (Psalms 118:24).

The Process

SERMON TITLE

Rev. Eason

DELIVERER OF THE MESSAGE

2|5|17

DATE

Scriptures Used: 2 Timothy 4:6-8

Notes

Solid Work Ethic
Gotta show up.
Healthy Lifestyle
Values and morals matters.

1. Leave it all on the field.
   All or nothing. 100% or 0%
   Give it my all.
2. Finish every down
   Finish the race - do not quit
   Thank God. Finish what you start.
   verse 7.
3. Don't give up.

SUMMARY (WHAT DID I LEARN):

CALL TO WORSHIP NOTE TAKER'S BOOK

Sankofa- Gods plan for
SERMON TITLE ourfuture.

Rev. Eason
DELIVERER OF THE MESSAGE

_2/26/17_
DATE

Scriptures Used: _Jeremian 29:11_

_____

Notes

"For I know the thoughts that
I think toward you, saith the
Lord, thoughts of peace and
not of evil, to give you an
expected end." -Jeremian 29:11

1. Vision of empowerment

2. Vision of evangelism

3. Vision of education
   II Timothy 2:15

4. Vision of ~~empathy~~ equality
   Luke

We are all made in an image and in the likeness of God.

All God's children treated w/ equality

SUMMARY (WHAT DID I LEARN):

Radical

SERMON TITLE

Rev. Eason

DELIVERER OF THE MESSAGE

5|7|17

DATE

Scriptures Used: _____

_____

Notes

People Orientated.

Meet the needs of others.

People are not perfect.

Filled with generosoty.

Spiritually Mature.

SUMMARY (WHAT DID I LEARN):

"This is the day that the Lord has made. Let us rejoice and be glad in it" (Psalms 118:24).

SERMON TITLE

DELIVERER OF THE MESSAGE

DATE

Scriptures Used: _____

_____

Notes

_____

_____

_____

_____

_____

_____

_____

_____

_____

_____

_____

_____

_____

_____

_____

_____

_____

_____

_____

_____

_____

_____

_____

_____

_____

_____

_____

_____

_____

_____

_____

_____

_____

_____

_____

SUMMARY (WHAT DID I LEARN):

_____

_____

_____

_____

_____

"This is the day that the Lord has made. Let us rejoice and be glad in it" (Psalms 118:24).

SERMON TITLE

_____

DELIVERER OF THE MESSAGE

_____

DATE

Scriptures Used: _____

_____

Notes

_____

_____

_____

_____

_____

_____

_____

_____

_____

_____

_____

_____

_____

_____

_____

_____

_____

_____

_____

_____

_____

_____

_____

_____

_____

_____

_____

_____

_____

_____

_____

_____

_____

SUMMARY (WHAT DID I LEARN):

_____

_____

_____

_____

_____

"This is the day that the Lord has made. Let us rejoice and be glad in it" (Psalms 118:24).

SERMON TITLE

DELIVERER OF THE MESSAGE

DATE

Scriptures Used: _____

_____

Notes

_____

_____

_____

_____

_____

_____

_____

_____

_____

_____

_____

_____

_____

_____

_____

_____

_____

_____

_____

_____

_____

_____

_____

_____

_____

_____

_____

_____

_____

_____

_____

_____

_____

SUMMARY (WHAT DID I LEARN):

_____

_____

_____

_____

_____

"This is the day that the Lord has made. Let us rejoice and be glad in it" (Psalms 118:24).

SERMON TITLE

DELIVERER OF THE MESSAGE

DATE

Scriptures Used: _____

_____

Notes

_____

_____

_____

_____

_____

_____

_____

_____

_____

_____

_____

_____

_____

_____

_____

_____

_____

_____

_____

_____

_____

_____

_____

_____

_____

_____

_____

_____

_____

_____

_____

_____

_____

_____

SUMMARY (WHAT DID I LEARN):

_____

_____

_____

_____

_____

"This is the day that the Lord has made. Let us rejoice and be glad in it" (Psalms 118:24).

SERMON TITLE

DELIVERER OF THE MESSAGE

DATE

Scriptures Used: _____

_____

Notes

_____

_____

_____

_____

_____

_____

_____

_____

_____

_____

_____

_____

_____

_____

_____

_____

_____

_____

_____

_____

_____

_____

_____

_____

_____

_____

_____

_____

_____

_____

_____

_____

_____

SUMMARY (WHAT DID I LEARN):

_____

_____

_____

_____

"This is the day that the Lord has made. Let us rejoice and be glad in it" (Psalms 118:24).

SERMON TITLE

DELIVERER OF THE MESSAGE

DATE

Scriptures Used: _____

_____

Notes

_____

_____

_____

_____

_____

_____

_____

_____

_____

_____

_____

_____

_____

_____

_____

_____

_____

_____

_____

_____

_____

_____

_____

_____

_____

_____

_____

_____

_____

_____

_____

_____

_____

SUMMARY (WHAT DID I LEARN):

_____

_____

_____

_____

_____

"This is the day that the Lord has made. Let us rejoice and be glad in it" (Psalms 118:24).

SERMON TITLE

DELIVERER OF THE MESSAGE

DATE

Scriptures Used: _____

_____

Notes

_____

_____

_____

_____

_____

_____

_____

_____

_____

_____

_____

_____

_____

_____

_____

_____

_____

_____

_____

_____

_____

_____

_____

_____

_____

_____

_____

_____

_____

_____

_____

_____

SUMMARY (WHAT DID I LEARN):

_____

_____

_____

_____

_____

"This is the day that the Lord has made. Let us rejoice and be glad in it" (Psalms 118:24).

SERMON TITLE

_____

DELIVERER OF THE MESSAGE

_____

DATE

Scriptures Used: _____

_____

Notes

_____
_____
_____
_____
_____
_____
_____
_____
_____
_____
_____
_____
_____
_____

_____
_____
_____
_____
_____
_____
_____
_____
_____
_____
_____
_____
_____
_____
_____
_____
_____
_____
_____

SUMMARY (WHAT DID I LEARN):

_____
_____
_____
_____

"This is the day that the Lord has made. Let us rejoice and be glad in it" (Psalms 118:24).

_____

SERMON TITLE

_____

DELIVERER OF THE MESSAGE

_____

DATE

Scriptures Used: _____

_____

Notes

_____

_____

_____

_____

_____

_____

_____

_____

_____

_____

_____

_____

_____

_____

_____

_____

_____

_____

_____

_____

_____

_____

_____

_____

_____

_____

_____

_____

_____

_____

_____

_____

SUMMARY (WHAT DID I LEARN):

_____

_____

_____

_____

"This is the day that the Lord has made. Let us rejoice and be glad in it" (Psalms 118:24).

SERMON TITLE

DELIVERER OF THE MESSAGE

DATE

Scriptures Used: _____

_____

Notes

_____

_____

_____

_____

_____

_____

_____

_____

_____

_____

_____

_____

_____

_____

_____

_____

_____

_____

_____

_____

_____

_____

_____

_____

_____

_____

_____

_____

_____

_____

_____

_____

SUMMARY (WHAT DID I LEARN):

_____

_____

_____

_____

_____

"This is the day that the Lord has made. Let us rejoice and be glad in it" (Psalms 118:24).

SERMON TITLE

DELIVERER OF THE MESSAGE

DATE

Scriptures Used: _____

_____

Notes

_____

_____

_____

_____

_____

_____

_____

_____

_____

_____

_____

_____

_____

_____

_____

_____

_____
_____
_____
_____
_____
_____
_____
_____
_____
_____
_____
_____
_____
_____
_____
_____
_____
_____
_____

SUMMARY (WHAT DID I LEARN):

_____
_____
_____
_____

"This is the day that the Lord has made. Let us rejoice and be glad in it" (Psalms 118:24).

SERMON TITLE

DELIVERER OF THE MESSAGE

DATE

Scriptures Used: _____

_____

Notes

_____

_____

_____

_____

_____

_____

_____

_____

_____

_____

_____

_____

_____

_____

_____

_____

_____

_____

_____

_____

_____

_____

_____

_____

_____

_____

_____

_____

_____

_____

_____

SUMMARY (WHAT DID I LEARN):

_____

_____

_____

_____

"This is the day that the Lord has made. Let us rejoice and be glad in it" (Psalms 118:24).

SERMON TITLE

DELIVERER OF THE MESSAGE

DATE

Scriptures Used: _____

_____

Notes

_____

_____

_____

_____

_____

_____

_____

_____

_____

_____

_____

_____

_____

_____

_____

_____

_____

_____

_____

_____

_____

_____

_____

_____

_____

_____

_____

_____

_____

_____

_____

_____

SUMMARY (WHAT DID I LEARN):

_____

_____

_____

_____

"This is the day that the Lord has made. Let us rejoice and be glad in it" (Psalms 118:24).

SERMON TITLE

DELIVERER OF THE MESSAGE

DATE

Scriptures Used: _____

_____

Notes

_____

_____

_____

_____

_____

_____

_____

_____

_____

_____

_____

_____

_____

_____

_____
_____
_____
_____
_____
_____
_____
_____
_____
_____
_____
_____
_____
_____
_____
_____
_____
_____
_____

SUMMARY (WHAT DID I LEARN):

_____
_____
_____
_____

"This is the day that the Lord has made. Let us rejoice and be glad in it" (Psalms 118:24).

SERMON TITLE

DELIVERER OF THE MESSAGE

DATE

Scriptures Used: _____

_____

Notes

_____
_____
_____
_____
_____
_____
_____
_____
_____
_____
_____
_____
_____
_____
_____
_____

_____

_____

_____

_____

_____

_____

_____

_____

_____

_____

_____

_____

_____

_____

_____

_____

_____

_____

_____

SUMMARY (WHAT DID I LEARN):

_____

_____

_____

_____

_____

"This is the day that the Lord has made. Let us rejoice and be glad in it" (Psalms 118:24).

SERMON TITLE

DELIVERER OF THE MESSAGE

DATE

Scriptures Used: _____

_____

Notes

_____

_____

_____

_____

_____

_____

_____

_____

_____

_____

_____

_____

_____

_____

_____

_____

_____

_____

_____

_____

_____

_____

_____

_____

_____

_____

_____

_____

_____

_____

_____

_____

_____

SUMMARY (WHAT DID I LEARN):

_____

_____

_____

_____

"This is the day that the Lord has made. Let us rejoice and be glad in it" (Psalms 118:24).

SERMON TITLE

DELIVERER OF THE MESSAGE

DATE

Scriptures Used: _____

_____

Notes

_____

_____

_____

_____

_____

_____

_____

_____

_____

_____

_____

_____

_____

_____

_____
_____
_____
_____
_____
_____
_____
_____
_____
_____
_____
_____
_____
_____
_____
_____
_____
_____
_____

SUMMARY (WHAT DID I LEARN):

_____
_____
_____
_____

"This is the day that the Lord has made. Let us rejoice and be glad in it" (Psalms 118:24).

SERMON TITLE

DELIVERER OF THE MESSAGE

DATE

Scriptures Used: _____

_____

Notes

_____

_____

_____

_____

_____

_____

_____

_____

_____

_____

_____

_____

_____

_____

_____

_____

_____

_____

_____

_____

_____

_____

_____

_____

_____

_____

_____

_____

_____

_____

_____

_____

SUMMARY (WHAT DID I LEARN):

_____

_____

_____

_____

_____

"This is the day that the Lord has made. Let us rejoice and be glad in it" (Psalms 118:24).

SERMON TITLE

DELIVERER OF THE MESSAGE

DATE

Scriptures Used: _____

_____

Notes

_____

_____

_____

_____

_____

_____

_____

_____

_____

_____

_____

_____

_____

_____

_____

_____

_____

_____

_____

_____

_____

_____

_____

_____

_____

_____

_____

_____

_____

_____

_____

_____

_____

_____

_____

SUMMARY (WHAT DID I LEARN):

_____

_____

_____

_____

"This is the day that the Lord has made. Let us rejoice and be glad in it" (Psalms 118:24).

SERMON TITLE

DELIVERER OF THE MESSAGE

DATE

Scriptures Used: _____

_____

Notes

_____
_____
_____
_____
_____
_____
_____
_____
_____
_____
_____
_____
_____
_____
_____

_____

_____

_____

_____

_____

_____

_____

_____

_____

_____

_____

_____

_____

_____

_____

_____

_____

_____

SUMMARY (WHAT DID I LEARN):

_____

_____

_____

_____

"This is the day that the Lord has made. Let us rejoice and be glad in it" (Psalms 118:24).

SERMON TITLE

DELIVERER OF THE MESSAGE

DATE

Scriptures Used: _____

_____

Notes

_____

_____

_____

_____

_____

_____

_____

_____

_____

_____

_____

_____

_____

_____

_____

_____

_____

_____

_____

_____

_____

_____

_____

_____

_____

_____

_____

_____

_____

_____

_____

_____

SUMMARY (WHAT DID I LEARN):

_____

_____

_____

_____

_____

"This is the day that the Lord has made. Let us rejoice and be glad in it" (Psalms 118:24).

SERMON TITLE

DELIVERER OF THE MESSAGE

DATE

Scriptures Used: _____

_____

Notes

_____

_____

_____

_____

_____

_____

_____

_____

_____

_____

_____

_____

_____

_____

_____

_____

_____

_____

_____

_____

_____

_____

_____

_____

_____

_____

_____

_____

_____

_____

_____

_____

_____

SUMMARY (WHAT DID I LEARN):

_____

_____

_____

_____

_____

"This is the day that the Lord has made. Let us rejoice and be glad in it" (Psalms 118:24).

SERMON TITLE

DELIVERER OF THE MESSAGE

DATE

Scriptures Used: _____

_____

Notes

_____

_____

_____

_____

_____

_____

_____

_____

_____

_____

_____

_____

_____

_____

_____

_____

_____

_____

_____

_____

_____

_____

_____

_____

_____

_____

_____

_____

_____

_____

SUMMARY (WHAT DID I LEARN):

_____

_____

_____

_____

_____

"This is the day that the Lord has made. Let us rejoice and be glad in it" (Psalms 118:24).

SERMON TITLE

DELIVERER OF THE MESSAGE

DATE

Scriptures Used: _____

_____

Notes

_____
_____
_____
_____
_____
_____
_____
_____
_____
_____
_____
_____
_____
_____
_____

_____
_____
_____
_____
_____
_____
_____
_____
_____
_____
_____
_____
_____
_____
_____
_____
_____

SUMMARY (WHAT DID I LEARN):

_____
_____
_____
_____

"This is the day that the Lord has made. Let us rejoice and be glad in it" (Psalms 118:24).

SERMON TITLE

DELIVERER OF THE MESSAGE

DATE

Scriptures Used: _____

_____

Notes

_____
_____
_____
_____
_____
_____
_____
_____
_____
_____
_____
_____
_____
_____
_____

SUMMARY (WHAT DID I LEARN):

"This is the day that the Lord has made. Let us rejoice and be glad in it" (Psalms 118:24).

SERMON TITLE

DELIVERER OF THE MESSAGE

DATE

Scriptures Used: _____

_____

Notes

_____

_____

_____

_____

_____

_____

_____

_____

_____

_____

_____

_____

_____

_____

_____

_____

_____

_____

_____

_____

_____

_____

_____

_____

_____

_____

_____

_____

_____

_____

_____

SUMMARY (WHAT DID I LEARN):

_____

_____

_____

_____

_____

"This is the day that the Lord has made. Let us rejoice and be glad in it" (Psalms 118:24).

SERMON TITLE

DELIVERER OF THE MESSAGE

DATE

Scriptures Used: _____

_____

Notes

_____

_____

_____

_____

_____

_____

_____

_____

_____

_____

_____

_____

_____

_____

_____

_____

_____

_____

_____

_____

_____

_____

_____

_____

_____

_____

_____

_____

_____

_____

SUMMARY (WHAT DID I LEARN):

_____

_____

_____

_____

"This is the day that the Lord has made. Let us rejoice and be glad in it" (Psalms 118:24).

SERMON TITLE

DELIVERER OF THE MESSAGE

DATE

Scriptures Used: _____

_____

Notes

_____

_____

_____

_____

_____

_____

_____

_____

_____

_____

_____

_____

_____

_____

_____

_____

_____

_____

_____

_____

_____

_____

_____

_____

_____

_____

_____

_____

_____

_____

_____

_____

_____

SUMMARY (WHAT DID I LEARN):

_____

_____

_____

_____

_____

"This is the day that the Lord has made. Let us rejoice and be glad in it" (Psalms 118:24).

SERMON TITLE

DELIVERER OF THE MESSAGE

DATE

Scriptures Used: _____

_____

Notes

_____

_____

_____

_____

_____

_____

_____

_____

_____

_____

_____

_____

_____

_____

_____
_____
_____
_____
_____
_____
_____
_____
_____
_____
_____
_____
_____
_____
_____
_____
_____
_____
_____

SUMMARY (WHAT DID I LEARN):

_____
_____
_____
_____

"This is the day that the Lord has made. Let us rejoice and be glad in it" (Psalms 118:24).

SERMON TITLE

DELIVERER OF THE MESSAGE

DATE

Scriptures Used: _____

_____

Notes

_____

_____

_____

_____

_____

_____

_____

_____

_____

_____

_____

_____

_____

_____

_____

_____

_____

_____

_____

_____

_____

_____

_____

_____

_____

_____

_____

_____

_____

_____

_____

_____

SUMMARY (WHAT DID I LEARN):

_____

_____

_____

_____

_____

"This is the day that the Lord has made. Let us rejoice and be glad in it" (Psalms 118:24).

SERMON TITLE

DELIVERER OF THE MESSAGE

DATE

Scriptures Used: _____

_____

Notes

_____

_____

_____

_____

_____

_____

_____

_____

_____

_____

_____

_____

_____

_____

_____

_____

_____

_____

_____

_____

_____

_____

_____

_____

_____

_____

_____

_____

_____

_____

_____

_____

_____

_____

_____

SUMMARY (WHAT DID I LEARN):

_____

_____

_____

_____

_____

"This is the day that the Lord has made. Let us rejoice and be glad in it" (Psalms 118:24).

SERMON TITLE

DELIVERER OF THE MESSAGE

DATE

Scriptures Used: _____

_____

Notes

_____
_____
_____
_____
_____
_____
_____
_____
_____
_____
_____
_____
_____
_____

_____

_____

_____

_____

_____

_____

_____

_____

_____

_____

_____

_____

_____

_____

_____

_____

_____

SUMMARY (WHAT DID I LEARN):

_____

_____

_____

_____

_____

"This is the day that the Lord has made. Let us rejoice and be glad in it" (Psalms 118:24).

SERMON TITLE

DELIVERER OF THE MESSAGE

DATE

Scriptures Used: _____

_____

Notes

_____

_____

_____

_____

_____

_____

_____

_____

_____

_____

_____

_____

_____

_____

_____

_____

_____

_____

_____

_____

_____

_____

_____

_____

_____

_____

_____

_____

_____

_____

_____

_____

_____

_____

SUMMARY (WHAT DID I LEARN):

_____

_____

_____

_____

_____

"This is the day that the Lord has made. Let us rejoice and be glad in it" (Psalms 118:24).

SERMON TITLE

DELIVERER OF THE MESSAGE

DATE

Scriptures Used: _____

_____

Notes

_____
_____
_____
_____
_____
_____
_____
_____
_____
_____
_____
_____
_____
_____

_____

_____

_____

_____

_____

_____

_____

_____

_____

_____

_____

_____

_____

_____

_____

_____

_____

_____

SUMMARY (WHAT DID I LEARN):

_____

_____

_____

_____

"This is the day that the Lord has made. Let us rejoice and be glad in it" (Psalms 118:24).

SERMON TITLE

DELIVERER OF THE MESSAGE

DATE

Scriptures Used: _____

_____

Notes

_____

_____

_____

_____

_____

_____

_____

_____

_____

_____

_____

_____

_____

_____

_____

_____

_____

_____

_____

_____

_____

_____

_____

_____

_____

_____

_____

_____

_____

_____

_____

_____

_____

_____

_____

SUMMARY (WHAT DID I LEARN):

_____

_____

_____

_____

"This is the day that the Lord has made. Let us rejoice and be glad in it" (Psalms 118:24).

SERMON TITLE

DELIVERER OF THE MESSAGE

DATE

Scriptures Used: _____

_____

Notes

_____
_____
_____
_____
_____
_____
_____
_____
_____
_____
_____
_____
_____
_____
_____

_____

_____

_____

_____

_____

_____

_____

_____

_____

_____

_____

_____

_____

_____

_____

_____

_____

_____

_____

_____

SUMMARY (WHAT DID I LEARN):

_____

_____

_____

_____

_____

"This is the day that the Lord has made. Let us rejoice and be glad in it" (Psalms 118:24).

SERMON TITLE

DELIVERER OF THE MESSAGE

DATE

Scriptures Used: _____

_____

Notes

_____
_____
_____
_____
_____
_____
_____
_____
_____
_____
_____
_____
_____
_____
_____
_____

_____

_____

_____

_____

_____

_____

_____

_____

_____

_____

_____

_____

_____

_____

_____

_____

_____

SUMMARY (WHAT DID I LEARN):

_____

_____

_____

_____

"This is the day that the Lord has made. Let us rejoice and be glad in it" (Psalms 118:24).

SERMON TITLE

DELIVERER OF THE MESSAGE

DATE

Scriptures Used: _____

_____

Notes

_____

_____

_____

_____

_____

_____

_____

_____

_____

_____

_____

_____

_____

_____

_____

_____

_____

_____

_____

_____

_____

_____

_____

_____

_____

_____

_____

_____

_____

_____

SUMMARY (WHAT DID I LEARN):

_____

_____

_____

_____

"This is the day that the Lord has made. Let us rejoice and be glad in it" (Psalms 118:24).

SERMON TITLE

DELIVERER OF THE MESSAGE

DATE

Scriptures Used: _____

_____

Notes

_____
_____
_____
_____
_____
_____
_____
_____
_____
_____
_____
_____
_____
_____
_____
_____

_____

_____

_____

_____

_____

_____

_____

_____

_____

_____

_____

_____

_____

_____

_____

_____

_____

SUMMARY (WHAT DID I LEARN):

_____

_____

_____

_____

_____

"This is the day that the Lord has made. Let us rejoice and be glad in it" (Psalms 118:24).

SERMON TITLE

DELIVERER OF THE MESSAGE

DATE

Scriptures Used: _____

_____

Notes

_____

_____

_____

_____

_____

_____

_____

_____

_____

_____

_____

_____

_____

_____

_____

_____

_____

_____

_____

_____

_____

_____

_____

_____

_____

_____

_____

_____

_____

_____

_____

SUMMARY (WHAT DID I LEARN):

_____

_____

_____

_____

_____

_____

"This is the day that the Lord has made. Let us rejoice and be glad in it" (Psalms 118:24).

SERMON TITLE

DELIVERER OF THE MESSAGE

DATE

Scriptures Used: _____

_____

Notes

_____

_____

_____

_____

_____

_____

_____

_____

_____

_____

_____

_____

_____

_____

_____

_____

_____

_____

_____

_____

_____

_____

_____

_____

_____

_____

_____

_____

_____

_____

_____

_____

_____

_____

_____

SUMMARY (WHAT DID I LEARN):

_____

_____

_____

_____

_____

"This is the day that the Lord has made. Let us rejoice and be glad in it" (Psalms 118:24).

SERMON TITLE

DELIVERER OF THE MESSAGE

DATE

Scriptures Used: _____

_____

Notes

_____

_____

_____

_____

_____

_____

_____

_____

_____

_____

_____

_____

_____

_____
_____
_____
_____
_____
_____
_____
_____
_____
_____
_____
_____
_____
_____
_____
_____
_____

SUMMARY (WHAT DID I LEARN):

_____
_____
_____
_____

"This is the day that the Lord has made. Let us rejoice and be glad in it" (Psalms 118:24).

_____

SERMON TITLE

_____

DELIVERER OF THE MESSAGE

_____

DATE

Scriptures Used: _____

_____

Notes

_____

_____

_____

_____

_____

_____

_____

_____

_____

_____

_____

_____

_____

_____

_____

_____

_____

_____

_____

_____

_____

_____

_____

_____

_____

_____

_____

_____

_____

_____

_____

_____

_____

SUMMARY (WHAT DID I LEARN):

_____

_____

_____

_____

_____

"This is the day that the Lord has made. Let us rejoice and be glad in it" (Psalms 118:24).

SERMON TITLE

DELIVERER OF THE MESSAGE

DATE

Scriptures Used: _____

_____

Notes

_____

_____

_____

_____

_____

_____

_____

_____

_____

_____

_____

_____

_____

_____

_____

_____

_____

_____

_____

_____

_____

_____

_____

_____

_____

_____

_____

_____

_____

_____

_____

_____

SUMMARY (WHAT DID I LEARN):

_____

_____

_____

_____

_____

_____

"This is the day that the Lord has made. Let us rejoice and be glad in it" (Psalms 118:24).

SERMON TITLE

DELIVERER OF THE MESSAGE

DATE

Scriptures Used: _____

_____

Notes

_____

_____

_____

_____

_____

_____

_____

_____

_____

_____

_____

_____

_____

_____

_____

_____

_____

_____

_____

_____

_____

_____

_____

_____

_____

_____

_____

_____

_____

_____

_____

_____

_____

SUMMARY (WHAT DID I LEARN):

_____

_____

_____

_____

_____

"This is the day that the Lord has made. Let us rejoice and be glad in it" (Psalms 118:24).

SERMON TITLE

DELIVERER OF THE MESSAGE

DATE

Scriptures Used: _____

_____

Notes

_____

_____

_____

_____

_____

_____

_____

_____

_____

_____

_____

_____

_____

_____

_____

_____

_____

_____

_____

_____

_____

_____

_____

_____

_____

_____

_____

_____

_____

_____

_____

SUMMARY (WHAT DID I LEARN):

_____

_____

_____

_____

_____

_____

"This is the day that the Lord has made. Let us rejoice and be glad in it" (Psalms 118:24).

SERMON TITLE

DELIVERER OF THE MESSAGE

DATE

Scriptures Used: _____

_____

Notes

_____

_____

_____

_____

_____

_____

_____

_____

_____

_____

_____

_____

_____

_____

_____

_____

_____

_____

_____

_____

_____

_____

_____

_____

_____

_____

_____

_____

_____

_____

_____

_____

_____

_____

SUMMARY (WHAT DID I LEARN):

_____

_____

_____

_____

"This is the day that the Lord has made. Let us rejoice and be glad in it" (Psalms 118:24).

SERMON TITLE

DELIVERER OF THE MESSAGE

DATE

Scriptures Used: _____

_____

Notes

_____

_____

_____

_____

_____

_____

_____

_____

_____

_____

_____

_____

_____

_____

_____

_____

_____

_____

_____

_____

_____

_____

_____

_____

_____

_____

_____

_____

_____

SUMMARY (WHAT DID I LEARN):

_____

_____

_____

_____

"This is the day that the Lord has made. Let us rejoice and be glad in it" (Psalms 118:24).

EXTRA NOTE SECTION
(BIBLE STUDY, MEETING, ETC.)

Notes

Notes

Notes

Notes

Notes

Notes

Notes

Notes

Notes

Notes

Notes

_____

_____

_____

_____

_____

_____

_____

_____

_____

_____

_____

_____

_____

_____

_____

_____

_____

_____

_____

_____

_____

_____

_____

_____

_____

_____

_____

Notes

Notes

_____

_____

_____

_____

_____

_____

_____

_____

_____

_____

_____

_____

_____

_____

_____

_____

_____

_____

_____

_____

_____

_____

_____

_____

_____

Notes

Notes

Notes

Notes

Notes

Notes

_____

_____

_____

_____

_____

_____

_____

_____

_____

_____

_____

_____

_____

_____

_____

_____

_____

_____

_____

_____

_____

_____

_____

_____

Notes

Notes

Notes

_____

_____

_____

_____

_____

_____

_____

_____

_____

_____

_____

_____

_____

_____

_____

_____

_____

_____

_____

_____

_____

Notes

Notes

Notes

Notes

_____

_____

_____

_____

_____

_____

_____

_____

_____

_____

_____

_____

_____

_____

_____

_____

_____

_____

_____

_____

_____

_____

Notes

Notes

Notes

_____

_____

_____

_____

_____

_____

_____

_____

_____

_____

_____

_____

_____

_____

_____

_____

_____

_____

_____

_____

_____

_____

_____

_____

Notes

Notes

_____

_____

_____

_____

_____

_____

_____

_____

_____

_____

_____

_____

_____

_____

_____

_____

_____

_____

_____

_____

_____

_____

_____

_____

Notes

SCRIPTURE
SECTIONS

Anger

Eph. 4:26-27

"Go ahead and be angry. You do well to be angry—but don't use your anger as fuel for revenge. And don't stay angry. Don't go to bed angry. Don't give the Devil that kind of foothold in your life."

Psalm 145: 8-9

The Lord is gracious and compassionate, slow to anger and rich in love.
The Lord is good to all; he has compassion on all he has made."

Proverbs 14:17

A quick-tempered man does foolish things, and a crafty man is hated.

Proverbs 15:18

A hot-tempered man stirs up dissension, but a patient man calms a quarrel.

Proverbs 16:32

Better a patient man than a warrior, a man who controls his temper than one who takes a city.

Proverbs 19:11

A man's wisdom gives him patience; it is to his glory to overlook an offense.

Proverbs 22:24-25

Do not make friends with a hot-tempered man, do not associate with one easily angered, or you may learn his ways and get yourself ensnared.

Proverbs 29:22

An angry man stirs up dissension and a hot-tempered one commits many sins.

Ecclesiastes 7:9

Do not quickly provoked in your spirit, for anger resides in the lap of fools.

Romans 12: 19-21

Do not take revenge, my friends, Believe room for God's wrath, for it is written: "it is my avenge; I will repay, "says the Lord. On the contrary; "if your enemy is hungry, feed him; if he is thirsty, give them something to drink. In doing this, you will heap burning coals on his head. "Do not be overcome by evil, but overcome evil with good."

Colossians 3:7-9

You used to walk in these ways, and the life you once lived. But now you must read your self of all such things as these: anger, rage, malice, slander, and filthy language from your lips. Do not lie to each other, since you have taken off your old self with its practices.

Colossians 3:21

Fathers, do not in bitter your children, or they will become discouraged.

Ephesians 4:25–27

Therefore each of you must put off falsehood and speak truthfully to his neighbor, for we are all members of one body. "in your anger do not sin:" do not let the sun go down while you are still angry, and do not give the devil foothold.

Ephesians 4:31–32

Get rid of all bitterness, rage and anger, brawling and slander, along with every form of malice. Be kind and compassionate to one another, forgiving each other, just as in Christ God forgave you.

2 Timothy 2:23–24

Don't have anything to do with foolish and stupid

arguments, because you know they produce quarrels. And the Lord' servant must not quarrel; instead, he must be kind to everyone, able to teach, not resentful.

~~~~~~~~~~~~

Blessed

Mathew 5:3-12

"Blessed are the poor in spirit,

for theirs is the kingdom of heaven.

Blessed are those who mourn,

for they will be comforted.

Blessed are the meek,

for they will inherit the earth.

Blessed are those who hunger and thirst for righteousness,

for they will be filled.

Blessed are the merciful,

for they will be shown mercy.

Blessed are the pure in heart,

for they will see God.

Blessed are the peacemakers,

for they will be called children of God.

Blessed are those who are persecuted because of righteousness,

for theirs is the kingdom of heaven.

"Blessed are you when people insult you, persecute you and falsely say all kinds of evil against you because of me.

Rejoice and be glad, because great is your reward in heaven, for in the same way they persecuted the prophets who were before you.

~~~~~~~~~~~~

Citizenship and Following Governing Authorities

Romans 13:1-7

Be a good citizen. All governments are under God. Insofar as there is peace and order, it's God's order. So live responsibly as a citizen. If you're irresponsible to the state, then you're irresponsible with God, and God will hold you responsible. Duly constituted authorities are only a threat if you're trying to get by with something. Decent citizens should have nothing to fear.

Do you want to be on good terms with the government? Be a responsible citizen and you'll get on just fine, the government working to your advantage. But if you're breaking the rules right and left, watch out. The police aren't there just to be admired in their uniforms. God also has an interest in keeping order, and he uses them to do it. That's why you must live responsibly—not just to avoid punishment but also because it's the right way to live.

That's also why you pay taxes—so that an orderly way

of life can be maintained. Fulfill your obligations as a citizen.
Pay your taxes, pay your bills, and respect your leaders.

Titus 3:1

Remind the people to respect the government and be
law-abiding, always ready to lend a helping hand. No insults,
no fights. God's people should be bighearted and courteous.

~~~~~~~~~~~~~

Cleanliness

2 Corinthians 7:1

Since we have these promises, dear friends, let us purify
ourselves from everything that contaminates body and spirit,
perfecting holiness out of reference for God.

~~~~~~~~~~~~~

Endurance

Luke 21:9-19

He said, "Watch out for the doomsday deceivers. Many
leaders are going to show up with forged identities claiming,
'I'm the One,' or, 'the end is near.' Don't fall for any of that.
When you hear of wars and uprisings, keep your head and don't
panic. This is routine history and no sign of the end."

He went on, "Nation will fight nation and ruler fight

ruler, over and over. Huge earthquakes will occur in various places. There will be famines. You'll think at times that the very sky is falling.

"But before any of this happens, they'll arrest you, hunt you down, and drag you to court and jail. It will go from bad to worse, dog-eat-dog, everyone at your throat because you carry my name. You'll end up on the witness stand, called to testify. Make up your mind right now not to worry about it. I'll give you the words and wisdom that will reduce all your accusers to stammers and stutters.

"You'll even be turned in by parents, brothers, relatives, and friends. Some of you will be killed. There's no telling who will hate you because of me. Even so, every detail of your body and soul—even the hairs of your head!—is in my care; nothing of you will be lost. Staying with it—that's what is required. Stay with it to the end. You won't be sorry; you'll be saved.

2 Timothy 2:1-7

So, my son, throw yourself into this work for Christ. Pass on what you heard from me—the whole congregation saying Amen!—to reliable leaders who are competent to teach others. When the going gets rough, take it on the chin with the rest of us, the way Jesus did. A soldier on duty doesn't get caught up in making deals at the marketplace. He concentrates on carrying out orders. An athlete who refuses to play by the rules will never get anywhere. It's the diligent farmer who gets the produce. Think it over. God will make it all plain.

~~~~~~~~~~~~~

Faithfulness

Lamentation 3:23-24

God's loyal love couldn't have run out, his merciful love couldn't have dried up. They're created new every morning. How great your faithfulness! I'm sticking with God (I say it over and over). He's all I've got left.

Mathew 25:23

The servant with the two thousand showed how he also had doubled his master's investment. His master commended him: 'Good work! You did your job well. From now on be my partner.'

Hebrews 13:7-8

Appreciate your pastoral leaders who gave you the Word of God. Take a good look at the way they live, and let their faithfulness instruct you, as well as their truthfulness. There should be a consistency that runs through us all. For

Jesus doesn't change—yesterday, today, tomorrow, he's always totally himself.

~~~~~~~~~~~~

Forgiveness

Mark 11:26

And when you assume the posture of prayer, remember that it's not all *asking.* If you have anything against someone, *forgive*—only then will your heavenly Father be inclined to also wipe your slate clean of sins."

Ephesians 4:31-32

Get rid of all bitterness, rage and anger, brawling and slander, along with every form of malice. Be kind and compassionate to one another, forgiving each other, just as in Christ God forgave you.

~~~~~~~~~~~~

Freedom

John 8:31-36

To the Jews who had believed him, Jesus said, "If you hold to my teaching, you are really my disciples. Then you will know the truth, and the truth will set you free."

They answered him, "We are Abraham's descendants and have never been slaves of anyone. How can you say that we shall be set free?"

Jesus replied, "Very truly I tell you, everyone who sins is a slave to sin. Now a slave has no permanent place in the family, but a son belongs to it forever. So if the Son sets you free, you will be free indeed.

~~~~~~~~~~~~

Fruitfulness

John 15:1-8

"I am the true vine, and my Father is the gardener. He cuts off every branch in me that bears no fruit, while every branch that does bear fruit he prunes so that it will be even more fruitful. You are already clean because of the word I have spoken to you. Remain in me, as I also remain in you. No branch can bear fruit by itself; it must remain in the vine. Neither can you bear fruit unless you remain in me.

"I am the vine; you are the branches. If you remain in me and I in you, you will bear much fruit; apart from me you can do nothing. If you do not remain in me, you are like a branch that is thrown away and withers; such branches are picked up, thrown into the fire and burned. If you remain in me and my words remain in you, ask whatever you wish, and it will be done for you. This is to my Father's glory, that you bear much fruit, showing yourselves to be my disciples.

Godliness

Titus 2:11-14

For the grace of God has appeared that offers salvation to all people. It teaches us to say "No" to ungodliness and worldly passions, and to live self-controlled, upright and godly lives in this present age, while we wait for the blessed hope— the appearing of the glory of our great God and Savior, Jesus Christ, who gave himself for us to redeem us from all wickedness and to purify for himself a people that are his very own, eager to do what is good.

I Timothy 4:8

For physical training is of some value, but godliness has value for all things, holding promise for both the present life and the life to come.

I Timothy 6:11

But you, man of God, flee from all this, and pursue righteousness, godliness, faith, love, endurance and gentleness.

~~~~~~~~~~~~~

Grief

Ecclesiastes 1:18

For with much wisdom comes much sorrow; the more knowledge, the more grief.

Psalm 22:24

For he has not despised or scorned

the suffering of the afflicted one;

he has not hidden his face from him

but has listened to his cry for help.

Psalm 30:5

For his anger lasts only a moment,

but his favor lasts a lifetime;

weeping may stay for the night,

but rejoicing comes in the morning.

I Thessalonians 4:13

Brothers and sisters, we do not want you to be uninformed about those who sleep in death, so that you do not grieve like the rest of mankind, who have no hope.

Revelation 21:4

He will wipe every tear from their eyes. There will be no more death' or mourning or crying or pain, for the old order of things has passed away.

~~~~~~~~~~~~~

God is our Strength

I Samuel 30:6

David was greatly distressed because the men were talking of stoning him; each one was bitter in spirit because of his sons and daughters. But David found strength in the Lord his God.

I Chronicles 16:11

Look to the Lord and his strength; seek his face always.

Psalm 27:1

The Lord is my light and my salvation—

whom shall I fear?

The Lord is the stronghold of my life—

of whom shall I be afraid?

Isaiah 40:28-31

Do you not know?

Have you not heard?

The Lord is the everlasting God,

the Creator of the ends of the earth.

He will not grow tired or weary,

and his understanding no one can fathom.

He gives strength to the weary

and increases the power of the weak.

Even youths grow tired and weary,

and young men stumble and fall;

but those who hope in the Lord

will renew their strength.

They will soar on wings like eagles;

they will run and not grow weary,

they will walk and not be faint.

Jeremiah 17:5

This is what the Lord says:

"Cursed is the one who trusts in man, who draws strength from mere flesh and whose heart turns away from the Lord.

2 Corinthians 12:9-10

But he said to me, "My grace is sufficient for you, for my power is made perfect in weakness." Therefore I will boast all the more gladly about my weaknesses, so that Christ's power may rest on me. That is why, for Christ's sake, I delight in weaknesses, in insults, in hardships, in persecutions, in difficulties. For when I am weak, then I am strong.

2 Timothy 4:17

But the Lord stood at my side and gave me strength, so that through me the message might be fully proclaimed and all the Gentiles might hear it. And I was delivered from the lion's mouth.

I Peter 4:11

If anyone speaks, they should do so as one who speaks the very words of God. If anyone serves, they should do so with the strength God provides, so that in all things God may be praised through Jesus Christ. To him be the glory and the power for ever and ever. Amen.

~~~~~~~~~~~~~

Happiness

Psalms 92:4

For You, O LORD, have made me glad by what You have done, I will sing for joy at the works of Your hands.

I Timothy 6:17

Instruct those who are rich in this present world not to be conceited or to fix their hope on the uncertainty of riches, but on God, who richly supplies us with all things to enjoy.

~~~~~~~~~~~~~

Hate

Psalms 97:10

Let those who love the Lord hate evil, for he guards the

lives of his faithful one and delivers them from the hand of the wicked.

Proverbs 6:16-19

There are six things the Lord hates, seven that are detestable to him:

haughty eyes,

a lying tongue,

hands that shed innocent blood,

a heart that devises wicked schemes,

feet that are quick to rush into evil,

a false witness who pours out lies

and a person who stirs up conflict in the community.

Hebrews 1:9

You have loved righteousness and hated wickedness; therefore God, your God, has set you above your companions by anointing you with the oil of joy."

~~~~~~~~~~~~~

Healing

Psalms 147:3

He heals the brokenhearted and binds up their wounds.

Proverbs 12:18

The words of the reckless pierce like swords, but the

tongue of the wise brings healing.

~~~~~~~~~~~~~

Holiness

1 Peter 1:13-16

Therefore, with minds that are alert and fully sober, set your hope on the grace to be brought to you when Jesus Christ is revealed at his coming. As obedient children, do not conform to the evil desires you had when you lived in ignorance. But just as he who called you is holy, so be holy in all you do; for it is written: "Be holy, because I am holy."

1 Thessalonians 4:6-7

For God did not call us to be impure, but to live a holy life.

Hebrews 12:14

Make every effort to live in peace with everyone and to be holy; without holiness no one will see the Lord.

~~~~~~~~~~~~~

Hope

1 Peter 1:13

Therefore, prepare your minds for action; be self-controlled; set your hope fully on the grace to be given you when Jesus Christ is revealed.

~~~~~~~~~~~~

Humility

Philippians 2:3-11

Do nothing out of selfish ambition or vain conceit. Rather, in humility value others above yourselves, not looking to your own interests but each of you to the interests of the others. In your relationships with one another, have the same mindset as Christ Jesus:

Who, being in very nature God, did not consider equality with God something to be used to his own advantage; rather, he made himself nothing by taking the very nature of a servant, being made in human likeness.

And being found in appearance as a man, he humbled himself by becoming obedient to death— even death on a cross!

Therefore God exalted him to the highest place and gave him the name that is above every name, that at the name of Jesus every knee should bow in heaven and on earth and under the earth, and every tongue acknowledge that Jesus Christ is Lord, to the glory of God the Father.

~~~~~~~~~~~~

Kindness

Proverbs 11:17

Those who are kind benefit themselves, but the cruel bring ruin on themselves.

Colossians 3:12-13

Therefore, as God's chosen people, holy and dearly loved, clothe yourselves with compassion, kindness, humility, gentleness and patience. Bear with each other and forgive one another if any of you has a grievance against someone. Forgive as the Lord forgave you.

Ephesians 4:32

Be kind and compassionate to one another, forgiving each other, just as in Christ God forgave you.

I Corinthians 13:4

Love is patient, love is kind. It does not envy, it does not boast, it is not proud.

~~~~~~~~~~~~

Labor

John 9:4

As long as it is day, we must do the works of him who

sent me. Night is coming, when no one can work.

~~~~~~~~~~~~~

Love

Luke 10:27

He answered, "'Love the Lord your God with all your heart and with all your soul and with all your strength and with all your mind'; and, 'Love your neighbor as yourself.'

1 Corinthians 13

If I speak in the tongues of men or of angels, but do not have love, I am only a resounding gong or a clanging cymbal. If I have the gift of prophecy and can fathom all mysteries and all knowledge, and if I have a faith that can move mountains, but do not have love, I am nothing. If I give all I possess to the poor and give over my body to hardship that I may boast, but do not have love, I gain nothing.

Love is patient, love is kind; It does not envy, it does not boast, it is not proud. It does not dishonor others, it is not self-seeking, it is not easily angered, it keeps no record of wrongs. Love does not delight in evil but rejoices with the truth. It always protects, always trusts, always hopes, always perseveres.

Love never fails. But where there are prophecies, they will cease; where there are tongues, they will be stilled; where there is knowledge, it will pass away. For we know in part and we prophesy in part, but when completeness comes, what is in part disappears. When I was a child, I talked like a child, I thought like a child, I reasoned like a child. When I became a man, I put the ways of childhood behind me. For now we see only a reflection as in a mirror; then we shall see face to face. Now I know in part; then I shall know fully, even as I am fully known.

And now these three remain: faith, hope and love. But the greatest of these is love.

Leviticus 19:18

Do not seek revenge or bear a grudge against anyone among your people, but love your neighbor as yourself. I am the Lord.

Galatians 5:6

For in Christ Jesus neither circumcision nor uncircumcision has any value. The only thing that counts is faith expressing itself through love.

~~~~~~~~~~~~~

Lust

Proverbs 5:3-5
For the lips of the adulterous woman drip honey,
and her speech is smoother than oil;
but in the end she is bitter as gall,
sharp as a double-edged sword.
Her feet go down to death;
her steps lead straight to the grave.

Mathew 5:27-28
You have heard that it was said, 'You shall not commit adultery.' But I tell you that anyone who looks at a woman lustfully has already committed adultery with her in his heart.

1 Thessalonians 4:5
not in passionate lust like the pagans, who do not know God;

James 1:14-15
...but each person is tempted when they are dragged away by their own evil desire and enticed. Then, after desire has conceived, it gives birth to sin; and sin, when it is full-grown, gives birth to death.

~~~~~~~~~~~~

Marriage

Genesis 2:24

That is why a man leaves his father and mother and is united to his wife, and they become one flesh.

Proverbs 5:15-19

Drink water from your own cistern,
running water from your own well.
Should your springs overflow in the streets,
your streams of water in the public squares?
Let them be yours alone,
never to be shared with strangers.
May your fountain be blessed,
and may you rejoice in the wife of your youth.
A loving doe, a graceful deer—
may her breasts satisfy you always,
may you ever be intoxicated with her love.

I Corinthians 7:9-39

But if they cannot control themselves, they should marry, for it is better to marry than to burn with passion.

To the married I give this command (not I, but the Lord): A wife must not separate from her husband. But if she does, she must remain unmarried or else be reconciled to her husband. And a husband must not divorce his wife.

To the rest I say this (I, not the Lord): If any brother has a wife who is not a believer and she is willing to live with him, he must not divorce her. And if a woman has a husband who is not a believer and he is willing to live with her, she must not divorce him. For the unbelieving husband has been sanctified through his wife, and the unbelieving wife has been sanctified through her believing husband. Otherwise your children would be unclean, but as it is, they are holy.

But if the unbeliever leaves, let it be so. The brother or the sister is not bound in such circumstances; God has called us to live in peace. How do you know, wife, whether you will save your husband? Or, how do you know, husband, whether you will save your wife?

~~~~~~~~~~~~~

Men

I Corinthians 10:13

No temptation has overtaken you except what is common to mankind. And God is faithful; he will not let you be tempted beyond what you can bear. But when you are tempted, he will also provide a way out so that you can endure it.

I Corinthians 7:33-34

But a married man is concerned about the affairs of this world—how he can please his wife—and his interests are divided. An unmarried woman or virgin is concerned about the Lord's affairs: Her aim is to be devoted to the Lord in both body and spirit. But a married woman is concerned about the affairs of this world—how she can please her husband.

Ephesians 5:23-33

For the husband is the head of the wife as Christ is the head of the church, his body, of which he is the Savior. Now as the church submits to Christ, so also wives should submit to their husbands in everything.

Husbands, love your wives, just as Christ loved the church and gave himself up for her to make her holy, cleansing her by the washing with water through the word, and to present her to himself as a radiant church, without stain or wrinkle or any other blemish, but holy and blameless. In this same way, husbands ought to love their wives as their own bodies. He who loves his wife loves himself. After all, no one ever hated their own body, but they feed and care for their body, just as Christ does the church for we are members of his body. "For this reason a man will leave his father and mother and be united to his wife, and the two will become one flesh." This is a profound mystery—but I am talking about Christ and the church. However, each one of you also must love his wife as he loves himself, and the wife must respect her husband.

I Corinthians 11:8-9, 11-12

For man did not come from woman, but woman from man; neither was man created for woman, but woman for man.

Nevertheless, in the Lord woman is not independent of man, nor is man independent of woman. For as woman came from man, so also man is born of woman. But everything comes from God.

Ephesians 6:4

Fathers, do not exasperate your children; instead, bring them up in the training and instruction of the Lord.

James 1:12-13

Blessed is the one who perseveres under trial because, having stood the test, that person will receive the crown of life that the Lord has promised to those who love him.

When tempted, no one should say, "God is tempting me." For God cannot be tempted by evil, nor does he tempt anyone;

I Peter 3:7

Husbands, in the same way be considerate as you live

with your wives, and treat them with respect as the weaker partner and as heirs with you of the gracious gift of life, so that nothing will hinder your prayers.

~~~~~~~~~~~~

Money

Exodus 22:25

If you lend money to one of my people among you who is needy, do not treat it like a business deal; charge no interest.

Deuteronomy 15:10

Give generously to them and do so without a grudging heart; then because of this the Lord your God will bless you in all your work and in everything you put your hand to.

Proverbs 12:11

He who works his land will abundant food, but he who chases fantasies lacks judgment.

Proverbs 12:11

Those who work their land will have abundant food, but those who chase fantasies have no sense.

Proverbs 13:11

Dishonest money dwindles away, but whoever gathers money little by little makes it grow.

Proverbs 22:9

The generous will themselves be blessed, for they share their food with the poor.

Proverbs 28:19

Those who work their land will have abundant food, but those who chase fantasies will have their fill of poverty.

Luke 10:7

Stay there, eating and drinking whatever they give you, for the worker deserves his wages. Do not move around from house to house.

Romans 13:7

Give to everyone what you owe them: If you owe taxes, pay taxes; if revenue, then revenue; if respect, then respect; if honor, then honor.

James 5:4

Look! The wages you failed to pay the workers who mowed your fields are crying out against you. The cries of the harvesters have reached the ears of the Lord Almighty.

~~~~~~~~~~~~~

Obedience

John 14:15-24

If you love me, keep my commands. And I will ask the Father, and he will give you another advocate to help you and be with you forever— the Spirit of truth. The world cannot accept him, because it neither sees him nor knows him. But you know him, for he lives with you and will be in you. I will not leave you as orphans; I will come to you. Before long, the world will not see me anymore, but you will see me. Because I live, you also will live. On that day you will realize that I am in my Father, and you are in me, and I am in you. Whoever has my commands and keeps them is the one who loves me. The one who loves me will be loved by my Father, and I too will love them and show myself to them."

Then Judas (not Judas Iscariot) said, "But, Lord, why do you intend to show yourself to us and not to the world?"

Jesus replied, "Anyone who loves me will obey my teaching. My Father will love them, and we will come to them and make our home with them. Anyone who does not love me will not obey my teaching. These words you hear are not my own; they belong to the Father who sent me.

1 Samuel 15:22

But Samuel replied: "Does the Lord delight in burnt offerings and sacrifices as much as in obeying the Lord? To obey is better than sacrifice, and to heed is better than the fat of rams.

Psalm 128:1

Blessed are all who fear the Lord, who walk in obedience to him.

Romans 1:5

Through him we received grace and apostleship to call all the Gentiles to the obedience that comes from faith for his name's sake.

Romans 6:16

Don't you know that when you offer yourselves to someone as obedient slaves, you are slaves of the one you obey—whether you are slaves to sin, which leads to death, or to obedience, which leads to righteousness?

2 John 1:6

And this is love: that we walk in obedience to his commands. As you have heard from the beginning, his command is that you walk in love.

~~~~~~~~~~~~

Perseverance

Mark 13:5-13

Jesus said to them: "Watch out that no one deceives you. Many will come in my name, claiming, 'I am he,' and will deceive many. When you hear of wars and rumors of wars, do not be alarmed. Such things must happen, but the end is still to come. Nation will rise against nation, and kingdom against kingdom. There will be earthquakes in various places, and famines. These are the beginning of birth pains.

"You must be on your guard. You will be handed over to the local councils and flogged in the synagogues. On account of me you will stand before governors and kings as witnesses to them. And the gospel must first be preached to all nations. Whenever you are arrested and brought to trial, do not worry beforehand about what to say. Just say whatever is given you at the time, for it is not you speaking, but the Holy Spirit.

"Brother will betray brother to death, and a father his child. Children will rebel against their parents and have them put to death. Everyone will hate you because of me, but the one who stands firm to the end will be saved.

Romans 5:3

Not only so, but we also glory in our sufferings,

because we know that suffering produces perseverance;

2 Thessalonians 3:5

May the Lord direct your hearts into God's love and Christ's perseverance.

Hebrews 12:1

Therefore, since we are surrounded by such a great cloud of witnesses, let us throw off everything that hinders and the sin that so easily entangles. And let us run with perseverance the race marked out for us, fixing our eyes on Jesus, the pioneer and perfecter of faith. For the joy set before him he endured the cross, scorning its shame, and sat down at the right hand of the throne of God.

James 1:3

Consider it pure joy, my brothers and sisters, whenever you face trials of many kinds, because you know that the testing of your faith produces perseverance. Let perseverance finish its work so that you may be mature and complete, not lacking anything.

~~~~~~~~~~~~

Prayer

Psalm 17:1

Hear me, Lord, my plea is just; listen to my cry. Hear my prayer— it does not rise from deceitful lips.

Psalm 17:6

I call on you, my God, for you will answer me; turn your ear to me and hear my prayer.

Proverbs 15:8

The Lord detests the sacrifice of the wicked, but the prayer of the upright pleases him.

Proverbs 28:9

If anyone turns a deaf ear to my instruction, even their prayers are detestable.

Mark 11:24

Therefore I tell you, whatever you ask for in prayer, believe that you have received it, and it will be yours.

Ephesians 6:18

And pray in the Spirit on all occasions with all kinds of prayers and requests. With this in mind, be alert and always keep on praying for all the Lord's people.

~~~~~~~~~~~~

Purity

You have heard that it was said, 'You shall not commit adultery.' But I tell you that anyone who looks at a woman lustfully has already committed adultery with her in his heart. If your right eye causes you to stumble, gouge it out and throw it away. It is better for you to lose one part of your body than for your whole body to be thrown into hell. And if your right hand causes you to stumble, cut it off and throw it away. It is better for you to lose one part of your body than for your whole body to go into hell.

1 Timothy 4:12

Don't let anyone look down on you because you are young, but set an example for the believers in speech, in conduct, in love, in faith and in purity.

2 Timothy 2:22

Flee the evil desires of youth and pursue righteousness, faith, love and peace, along with those who call on the Lord out of a pure heart.

~~~~~~~~~~~~

Reading The Bible

John 5:39-40

You study the Scriptures diligently because you think that in them you have eternal life. These are the very Scriptures that testify about me, yet you refuse to come to me to have life.

Psalm 1:1-2

Blessed is the one

who does not walk in step with the wicked

or stand in the way that sinners take

or sit in the company of mockers,

but whose delight is in the law of the Lord,

and who meditates on his law day and night.

Ephesians 6:10-18

Finally, be strong in the Lord and in his mighty power. Put on the full armor of God, so that you can take your stand against the devil's schemes. For our struggle is not against flesh and blood, but against the rulers, against the authorities, against the powers of this dark world and against the spiritual forces of evil in the heavenly realms. Therefore put on the full armor of God, so that when the day of evil comes, you may be able to stand your ground, and after you have done everything, to stand. Stand firm then, with the belt of truth buckled around your waist, with the breastplate of righteousness in place, and with your feet fitted with the readiness that comes from the gospel of peace. In addition to all this, take up the shield of faith, with which you can extinguish all the flaming arrows of the evil one. Take the helmet of salvation and the sword of the Spirit, which is the word of God.

And pray in the Spirit on all occasions with all kinds of prayers and requests. With this in mind, be alert and always keep on praying for all the Lord's people.

~~~~~~~~~~~~~

Righteousness

Psalms 85:10

Love and faithfulness meet together; righteousness and peace kiss each other.

Mathew 5:6

Blessed are those who hunger and thirst for righteousness, for they will be filled.

Mathew 6:33

But seek first his kingdom and his righteousness, and all these things will be given to you as well.

Proverbs 11:6

The righteousness of the upright delivers them, but the unfaithful are trapped by evil desires.

Isaiah 32:17

The fruit of that righteousness will be peace; its effect will be quietness and confidence forever.

Mathew 5:6

Blessed are those who hunger and thirst for righteousness, for they will be filled.

Mathew 6:33

But seek first his kingdom and his righteousness, and all these things will be given to you as well.

Romans 4:5

However, to the one who does not work but trusts God who justifies the ungodly, their faith is credited as righteousness.

Romans 6:18

You have been set free from sin and have become slaves to righteousness.

2 Corinthians 5:21

God made him who had no sin to be sin for us, so that in him we might become the righteousness of God.

Galatians 2:21

I do not set aside the grace of God, for if righteousness could be gained through the law, Christ died for nothing!"

1 Timothy 6:11

But you, man of God, flee from all this, and pursue righteousness, godliness, faith, love, endurance and gentleness.

~~~~~~~~~~~~

Stewardship

I Corinthians 4:2

Now it is required that those who have been given a trust must prove faithful.

2 Corinthians 9:6-7

Remember this: Whoever sows sparingly will also reap sparingly, and whoever sows generously will also reap generously. Each of you should give what you have decided in your heart to give, not reluctantly or under compulsion, for God loves a cheerful giver.

~~~~~~~~~~~~

Truthfulness

Job 27:4

...as long as I have life within me, the breath of God in my nostrils, my lips will not say anything wicked, and my tongue will not utter lies.

Proverbs 4:23-27

Above all else, guard your heart,

for everything you do flows from it.

Keep your mouth free of perversity;

keep corrupt talk far from your lips.

Let your eyes look straight ahead;

fix your gaze directly before you.

Give careful thought to the paths for your feet

and be steadfast in all your ways.

Do not turn to the right or the left;

keep your foot from evil.

Proverbs 10:9

Whoever walks in integrity walks securely, but whoever takes crooked paths will be found out.

Proverbs 12:17

An honest witness tells the truth, but a false witness

tells lies.

Proverbs 21:15

When justice is done, it brings joy to the righteous but terror to evildoers.

Romans 12:17

Do not repay anyone evil for evil. Be careful to do what is right in the eyes of everyone.

2 Corinthians 4:1-2

Therefore, since through God's mercy we have this ministry, we do not lose heart. Rather, we have renounced secret and shameful ways; we do not use deception, nor do we distort the word of God. On the contrary, by setting forth the truth plainly we commend ourselves to everyone's conscience in the sight of God.

2 Corinthians 8:21

For we are taking pains to do what is right, not only in the eyes of the Lord but also in the eyes of man.

Ephesians 4:14-16

Then we will no longer be infants, tossed back and forth by the waves, and blown here and there by every wind of

184 *CALL TO WORSHIP NOTE TAKER'S BOOK*

teaching and by the cunning and craftiness of people in their deceitful scheming. Instead, speaking the truth in love, we will grow to become in every respect the mature body of him who is the head, that is, Christ. From him the whole body, joined and held together by every supporting ligament, grows and builds itself up in love, as each part does its work.

Titus 1:7

Since an overseer manages God's household, he must be blameless—not overbearing, not quick-tempered, not given to drunkenness, not violent, not pursuing dishonest gain.

I Peter 3:16

But in your hearts revere Christ as Lord. Always be prepared to give an answer to everyone who asks you to give the reason for the hope that you have. But do this with gentleness and respect, keeping a clear conscience, so that those who speak maliciously against your good behavior in Christ may be ashamed of their slander.

I John 1:8-10

If we claim to be without sin, we deceive ourselves and the truth is not in us. If we confess our sins, he is faithful and just and will forgive us our sins and purify us from all unrighteousness. If we claim we have not sinned, we make him out to be a liar and his word is not in us.

~~~~~~~~~~~~

Trust

Psalm 37:3-5

Trust in the Lord and do good;

  dwell in the land and enjoy safe pasture.

Take delight in the Lord,

  and he will give you the desires of your heart.

Commit your way to the Lord;

  trust in him and he will do this:

Proverbs 3:5-6

Trust in the Lord with all your heart and lean not on your own understanding; in all your ways submit to him, and he will make your paths straight.

Ephesians 4:14-15

Then we will no longer be infants, tossed back and forth by the waves, and blown here and there by every wind of teaching and by the cunning and craftiness of people in their deceitful scheming. Instead, speaking the truth in love, we will grow to become in every respect the mature body of him who is the head, that is, Christ.

Philippians 4:8-9

Finally, brothers and sisters, whatever is true, whatever is noble, whatever is right, whatever is pure, whatever is lovely, whatever is admirable—if anything is excellent or praiseworthy—think about such things. Whatever you have learned or received or heard from me, or seen in me—put it into practice. And the God of peace will be with you.

I Corinthians 4:2

Now it is required that those who have been given a trust must prove faithful.

~~~~~~~~~~~~

Watchfulness

Mark 13:34-37

It's like a man going away: He leaves his house and puts his servants in charge, each with their assigned task, and tells the one at the door to keep watch.

"Therefore keep watch because you do not know when the owner of the house will come back—whether in the evening, or at midnight, or when the rooster crows, or at dawn. If he comes suddenly, do not let him find you sleeping. What I say to you, I say to everyone: 'Watch!'"

Luke 12:35-37

Be dressed ready for service and keep your lamps burning, like servants waiting for their master to return from a wedding banquet, so that when he comes and knocks they can immediately open the door for him. It will be good for those servants whose master finds them watching when he comes.

~~~~~~~~~~~~~

Worship

John 4:23-24

Yet a time is coming and has now come when the true worshipers will worship the Father in the Spirit and in truth, for they are the kind of worshipers the Father seeks. God is spirit, and his worshipers must worship in the Spirit and in truth.

Psalm 86:9

All the nations you have made will come and worship before you, Lord; they will bring glory to your name.

Psalm 95:6

Come, let us bow down in worship, let us kneel before the Lord our Maker;

Psalms 96:9

Worship the Lord in the splendor of his holiness; tremble before him, all the earth.

Jeremiah 13:10

These wicked people, who refuse to listen to my words, who follow the stubbornness of their hearts and go after other gods to serve and worship them, will be like this belt— completely useless!

John 4:24

God is spirit, and his worshipers must worship in the Spirit and in truth."

~~~~~~~~~~~~

Women

Proverbs 12:4

A wife of noble character is her husband's crown, but a disgraceful wife is like decay in his bones.

Proverbs 31:10-36

A wife of noble character who can find?

She is worth far more than rubies.

Her husband has full confidence in her

and lacks nothing of value.

She brings him good, not harm,

all the days of her life.

She selects wool and flax

and works with eager hands.

She is like the merchant ships,

    bringing her food from afar.

She gets up while it is still night;

    she provides food for her family

    and portions for her female servants.

She considers a field and buys it;

    out of her earnings she plants a vineyard.

She sets about her work vigorously;

    her arms are strong for her tasks.

She sees that her trading is profitable,

    and her lamp does not go out at night.

In her hand she holds the distaff

    and grasps the spindle with her fingers.

She opens her arms to the poor

    and extends her hands to the needy.

When it snows, she has no fear for her household;

    for all of them are clothed in scarlet.

She makes coverings for her bed;

    she is clothed in fine linen and purple.

Her husband is respected at the city gate,

    where he takes his seat among the elders of the land.

She makes linen garments and sells them,

    and supplies the merchants with sashes.

She is clothed with strength and dignity;

she can laugh at the days to come.

She speaks with wisdom,

and faithful instruction is on her tongue.

She watches over the affairs of her household

and does not eat the bread of idleness.

Her children arise and call her blessed;

her husband also, and he praises her:

"Many women do noble things,

but you surpass them all."

Charm is deceptive, and beauty is fleeting;

but a woman who fears the Lord is to be praised.

Honor her for all that her hands have done,

and let her works bring her praise at the city gate.

Luke 8:2-3

After this, Jesus traveled about from one town and village to another, proclaiming the good news of the kingdom of God. The Twelve were with him, and also some women who had been cured of evil spirits and diseases: Mary (called Magdalene) from whom seven demons had come out; Joanna the wife of Chuza, the manager of Herod's household; Susanna; and many others. These women were helping to support them out of their own means.

Ephesians 5:22-33

Wives, submit yourselves to your own husbands as you do to the Lord. For the husband is the head of the wife as Christ is the head of the church, his body, of which he is the Savior. Now as the church submits to Christ, so also wives should submit to their husbands in everything.

Husbands, love your wives, just as Christ loved the church and gave himself up for her to make her holy, cleansing her by the washing with water through the word, and to present her to himself as a radiant church, without stain or wrinkle or any other blemish, but holy and blameless. In this same way, husbands ought to love their wives as their own bodies. He who loves his wife loves himself. After all, no one ever hated their own body, but they feed and care for their body, just as Christ does the church for we are members of his body. "For this reason a man will leave his father and mother and be united to his wife, and the two will become one flesh." This is a profound mystery—but I am talking about Christ and the church. However, each one of you also must love his wife as he loves himself, and the wife must respect her husband.

I Peter 3:1-6

Wives, in the same way submit yourselves to your own husbands so that, if any of them do not believe the word, they may be won over without words by the behavior of their wives, when they see the purity and reverence of your lives. Your beauty should not come from outward adornment, such as elaborate hairstyles and the wearing of gold jewelry or fine clothes. Rather, it should be that of your inner self, the unfading beauty of a gentle and quiet spirit, which is of great worth in God's sight. For this is the way the holy women of the past who put their hope in God used to adorn themselves. They submitted themselves to their own husbands, like Sarah, who obeyed Abraham and called him her lord. You are her daughters if you do what is right and do not give way to fear.

Titus 2:3-5

Likewise, teach the older women to be reverent in the way they live, not to be slanderers or addicted too much wine, but to teach what is good. Then they can urge the younger women to love their husbands and children, to be self-controlled and pure, to be busy at home, to be kind, and to be subject to their husbands, so that no one will malign the word of God.

~~~~~~~~~~~~

Worry

Mathew 6:25-34

Therefore I tell you, do not worry about your life, what you will eat or drink; or about your body, what you will wear.

Is not life more than food, and the body more than clothes? Look at the birds of the air; they do not sow or reap or store away in barns, and yet your heavenly Father feeds them. Are you not much more valuable than they? Can any one of you by worrying add a single hour to your life?

"And why do you worry about clothes? See how the flowers of the field grow. They do not labor or spin. Yet I tell you that not even Solomon in all his splendor was dressed like one of these. If that is how God clothes the grass of the field, which is here today and tomorrow, is thrown into the fire, will he not much more clothe you—you of little faith? So do not worry, saying, 'What shall we eat?' or 'What shall we drink?' or 'What shall we wear?' For the pagans run after all these things, and your heavenly Father knows that you need them. 33 But seek first his kingdom and his righteousness, and all these things will be given to you as well. Therefore do not worry about tomorrow, for tomorrow will worry about itself. Each day has enough trouble of it's own.

John 14:27

Peace I leave with you; my peace I give you. I do not give to you as the world gives. Do not let your hearts be troubled and do not be afraid.

Philippians 4:6

Do not be anxious about anything, but in every situation, by prayer and petition, with thanksgiving, present your requests to God.

~~~~~~~~~~~~

Uplifting Scriptures

Philippians 4:13

I can do all this through him who gives me strength.

2 Timothy 1:7

For the Spirit God gave us does not make us timid, but gives us power, love and self-discipline.

Romans 12:3

For by the grace given me I say to every one of you: Do not think of yourself more highly than you ought, but rather think of yourself with sober judgment, in accordance with the faith God has distributed to each of you.

Daniel 11:32

With flattery he will corrupt those who have violated the covenant, but the people who know their God will firmly resist him.

I John 4:4

You, dear children, are from God and have overcome them, because the one who is in you is greater than the one who is in the world.

2 Corinthians 2:14

But thanks be to God, who always leads us as captives in Christ's triumphal procession and uses us to spread the aroma of the knowledge of him everywhere.

Mathew 8:17

This was to fulfill what was spoken through the prophet Isaiah: "He took up our infirmities and bore our diseases."

I Corinthians 3:17

If anyone destroys God's temple, God will destroy that person; for God's temple is sacred, and you together are that temple.

I Peter 5:7

Cast all your anxiety on him because he cares for you.

Romans 8:1

Therefore, there is now no condemnation for those who are in Christ Jesus, because through Christ Jesus the law of the Spirit who gives life has set you free from the law of sin and death.

Galatians 3:13-14

Christ redeemed us from the curse of the law by becoming a curse for us, for it is written: "Cursed is everyone who is hung on a pole." He redeemed us in order that the blessing given to Abraham might come to the Gentiles through Christ Jesus, so that by faith we might receive the promise of the Spirit.

Philippians 4:11

I am not saying this because I am in need, for I have learned to be content whatever the circumstances.

2 Corinthians 5:21

God made him who had no sin to be sin for us, so that in him we might become the righteousness of God.

1 Corinthians 2:12

What we have received is not the spirit of the world, but the Spirit who is from God, so that we may understand what God has freely given us.

Proverbs 3:24-26

When you lie down, you will not be afraid;

when you lie down, your sleep will be sweet.

Have no fear of sudden disaster

or of the ruin that overtakes the wicked,

for the Lord will be at your side

and will keep your foot from being snared.

Romans 8:37

No, in all these things we are more than conquerors through him who loved us.

Isaiah 26:3

You will keep in perfect peace those whose minds are steadfast, because they trust in you.

John 16:33

"I have told you these things, so that in me you may have peace. In this world you will have trouble. But take heart! I have overcome the world."

I Corinthians 2:9-10

However, as it is written:

"What no eye has seen, what no ear has heard and what no human mind has conceived" the things God has prepared for those who love him these are the things God has revealed to us by his Spirit.

The Spirit searches all things, even the deep things of God.

About the Author

Nancy Roundtree – author, speaker, mother, and educator. She has a unique passion for mentoring young and older women and children through education. Her approach is to use and show how Bible scriptures bring life to everyday struggles, as well as offer support and encouragement during deliverances.

She is the best selling author of Call To Worship Note Taker's Book, Beyond Sunday… Dangerously Distracted, and Prayer Journal.

Nancy holds a Bachelors degree from Life University and a Masters from Liberty University in Educational Leadership.

Currently, she resides right outside of the Atlanta Metro area. She has taught elementary and Sunday School, mentored and tutored many throughout the years. Follow her at:

Email: Blessed@NancyRoundtree.com

Twitter: @NancyMRoundtree

@CallToWorshipNotetakersbook

Website: www.NancyRoundtree.com

Also check out other titles by this author:

Beyond Sunday… Dangerously Distracted

Prayer Journal